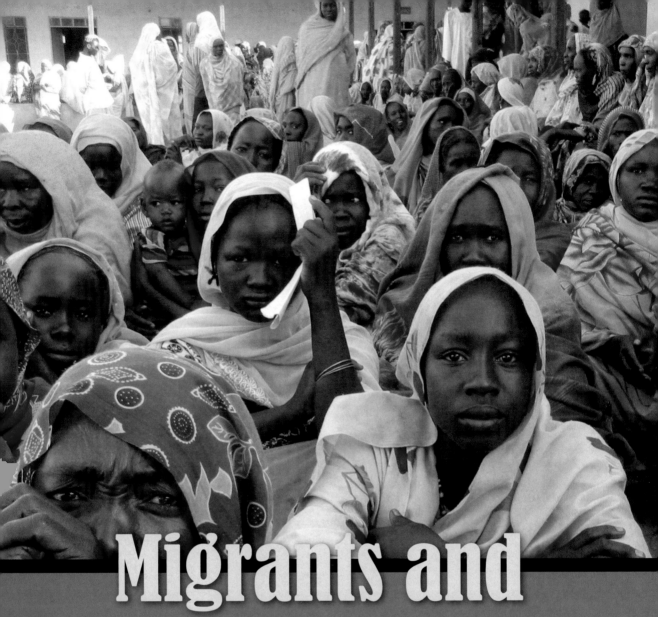

Migrants and Refugees

Edited by Aaron Carr

www.av2books.com

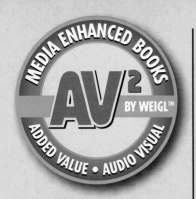

AV² provides enriched content that supplements and complements this book. Weigl's AV² books strive to create inspired learning and engage young minds in a total learning experience.

Your AV² Media Enhanced books come alive with...

Audio
Listen to sections of the book read aloud.

Key Words
Study vocabulary, and complete a matching word activity.

Go to **www.av2books.com,** and enter this book's unique code.

BOOK CODE

V180169

AV² **by Weigl** brings you media enhanced books that support active learning.

Download the AV² catalog at **www.av2books.com/catalog**

Video
Watch informative video clips.

Quizzes
Test your knowledge.

Embedded Weblinks
Gain additional information for research.

Slide Show
View images and captions, and prepare a presentation.

Try This!
Complete activities and hands-on experiments.

... and much, much more!

AV² Online Navigation on page 48

Published by AV² by Weigl
350 5th Avenue, 59th Floor
New York, NY 10118

Websites: www.av2books.com   www.weigl.com

Copyright ©2015 AV² by Weigl
All rights reserved. No part of this publication may be reproduced, stored in a retrieval system, or transmitted in any form or by any means, electronic, mechanical, photocopying, recording, or otherwise, without the prior written permission of the publisher.

Library of Congress Control Number: 2014940094

ISBN 978-1-4896-1106-2 (hardcover)
ISBN 978-1-4896-1107-9 (softcover)
ISBN 978-1-4896-1108-6 (single-user eBook)
ISBN 978-1-4896-1109-3 (multi-user eBook)

Printed in the United States of America in Brainerd, Minnesota
2 3 4 5 6 7 8 9 0   20 19 18 17 16

032016
080316

Weigl acknowledges Getty Images as its primary image supplier for this title.

Every reasonable effort has been made to trace ownership and to obtain permission to reprint copyright material. The publishers would be pleased to have any errors or omissions brought to their attention so that they may be corrected in subsequent printings.

Project Coordinator: Aaron Carr
Art Director: Terry Paulhus

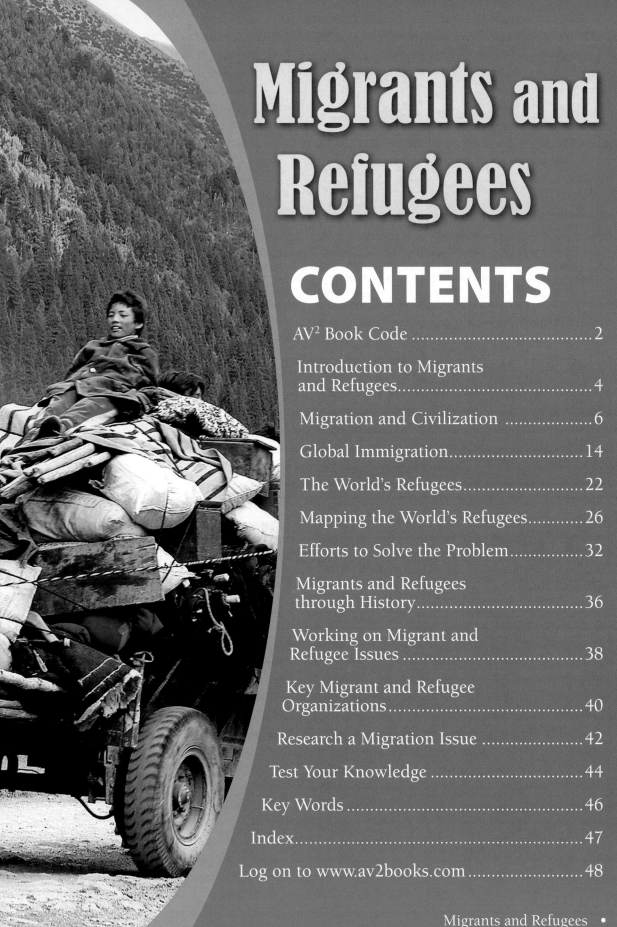

Migrants and Refugees

CONTENTS

Introduction to Migrants and Refugees

Every year, millions of people move from their homes and communities. Some leave looking for a better life. They move to find work or go to school. Others flee from their homes because of war, **persecution**, or disaster. People who move by choice are called migrants or immigrants. People who are forced from their homes are known as refugees.

Migration and Civilization

"Humans have always been on the move. Migrations have changed the course of history."

Global Immigration

"Immigrants make important contributions to their new countries."

The World's Refugees

Efforts to Solve the Problem

"The number of refugees created by natural disasters is small compared to the number resulting from war."

"The goal for many refugees is to return home. Before they can return, the situation inside their homeland must be safe."

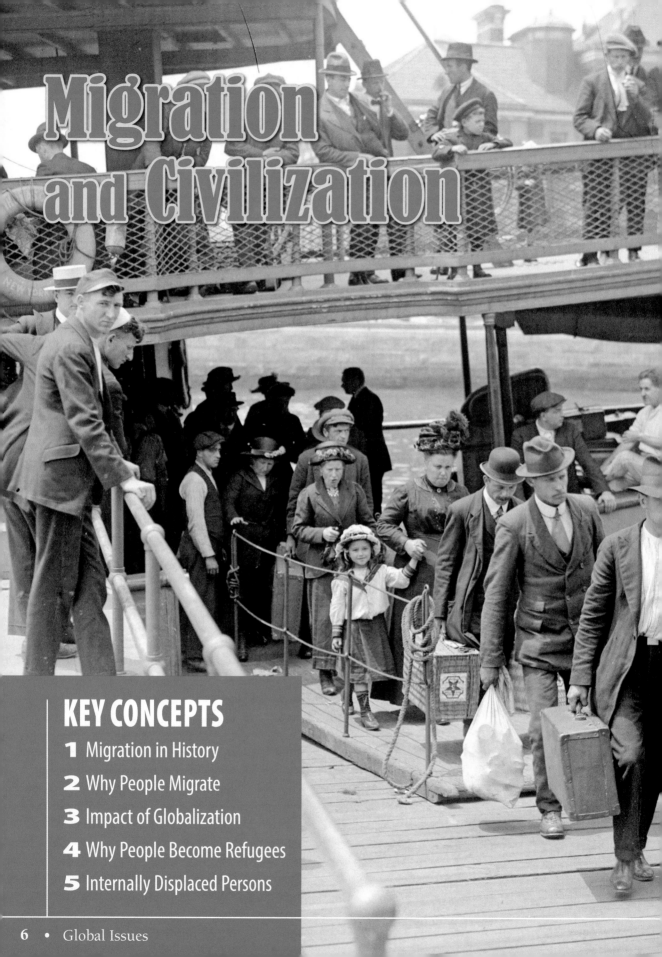

Migration and Civilization

KEY CONCEPTS

Humans have always been on the move. About 60,000 years ago, early humans in search of food walked out of Africa and began to live in other parts of the world. People have not stopped moving since.

1 Migration in History

Migrations have changed the course of history. The event known as the Great Atlantic Migration of the 1800s and early 1900s helped make the United States a powerful nation. During that time, millions of immigrants to the United States left Europe and crossed the Atlantic Ocean by ship. Most of them were seeking better jobs and incomes. Some left their homes to escape persecution for their political or religious beliefs. Many immigrants found jobs in factories, helping U.S. industries to grow. Some helped build roads, bridges, and the first skyscrapers.

The upheavals of World War II (1939–1945) led to large-scale migrations. After the war, thousands of European Jews who survived the **Holocaust** migrated to the Middle East. They helped create the modern state of Israel.

In 1947, what had been the British colony of India was partitioned, or divided, into the independent countries of India and Pakistan. Most people in the country of India followed the Hindu faith. Most

Pakistanis were Muslims, or followers of the religion Islam. About 10 million to 15 million people decided to resettle rather than live in a country where they were a religious minority. Hindus in Pakistan moved to India in large numbers, while millions of Muslims in India moved to Pakistan.

Countries with the Most Immigrants, 2013

Some countries attract more immigrants than others. These nations may have more jobs available or fewer restrictions on who can enter the country.

United States
Russia
Germany
Saudi Arabia
United Arab Emirates
Great Britain
France
Canada
Australia
Spain

0   10   20   30   40   50
millions of people

2 Why People Migrate

Finding work or better-paying work is a common reason why people migrate. Recent events in China are an example. Many people in **rural** China struggle to survive on earnings of about $2 per day. Over the past 30 years, more than 260 million rural Chinese have moved to China's cities, often to look for work in factories. This has been one of the largest migrations in history.

Persecution for religious beliefs often forces people from their homes. The Puritans left England and Holland for North America in the 1600s because of religious **intolerance**. When the Nazis came to power in Germany in the 1930s, they persecuted that country's Jewish population. Some Jews were able to flee to other nations before the Holocaust began.

Others migrate for social reasons. They move to be closer to family or friends. Some people migrate after a natural disaster has changed the area in which they lived.

Still others are forced to migrate. During the 19th century, the U.S. government forced many American Indians onto **reservations**, often far from their traditional homes. The government wanted to make way for new European-American settlements in the West.

In 2013, about 232 million people worldwide lived in a country different from the one in which they were born. This was a higher number of international migrants than at any earlier time in history. According to the United Nations (UN), 3.2 percent of the world's people were international migrants in 2013.

The Pilgrims who landed at what is now Plymouth, Massachusetts, migrated in order to practice their religion freely.

Should Countries Stop Immigrants from Using Government Programs?

Often, immigrants wish to take part in government assistance programs in their new countries. These programs may include health care, payments to people who are out of work, and financial aid to help poor people pay for food or housing. Some people oppose spending government money to help immigrants.

Some Politicians
Immigrants should not be able to take part in government assistance programs. If they are allowed to do so, that encourages people to come to the country for the wrong reasons. People will immigrate not to work, but just to receive government aid.

Some Taxpayers
The money for government assistance programs comes from the taxes citizens pay. If large numbers of immigrants take part in these programs, taxes may have to be increased. I feel sad for immigrant families that are having a difficult time. However, I do not think citizens should be required to pay for helping them.

Public Policy Researchers
Research shows that very few immigrants come to a country to receive government benefits. They are much more likely to come seeking work. In addition, the largest portion of the money spent in government assistance programs goes to older people. On average, immigrants tend to be young. They are not in the age group likely to need the most aid.

Immigration Activists
Immigrants bring ideas and skills to their new country. They help that country's economy grow. If they need some assistance when they first arrive, that is money well spent. Over time, these people will become taxpayers and make the country stronger.

| For | Supportive | Undecided | Unsupportive | Against |

3 Impact of Globalization

By the 21st century, **globalization** had reached many parts of the world. People could travel and communicate easily over large distances. Products of all kinds could be shipped from one continent to another quickly and cheaply. As a result, goods, services, and people often move across national borders.

Globalization is not new. Nearly 2,000 years ago, Europeans traveled to China and other Asian nations. They traded goods such as grapes and cotton for silk, spices, and other Asian products to bring back to Europe. Each region prospered.

In recent years, globalization has made it easier for people travel to other countries in search of work. Immigrants often prefer going to **developed countries**, especially in Europe and North America. Europe is the most common destination, with 72 million international migrants in 2013. The country with the largest number of such migrants is the United States. It had 45.8 million.

Globalization involves both skilled and untrained workers. For example, in recent years, there has been a shortage of nurses in the United States. As a result, thousands of nurses from the Philippines have immigrated to the United States. They find work that is not available in their homeland. In some American hospitals, Filipino nurses make up a majority of the staff.

About half of all nurses from other countries coming to work in the United States are from the Philippines.

Many Rwandan refugees in 1994 were housed in camps in nearby Tanzania.

4 Why People Become Refugees

Millions of people around the world are refugees. According to the United Nations High Commissioner for Refugees (UNHCR), by the end of 2012, there were about 15.4 million refugees worldwide. Of that number, 937,000 people sought **asylum**.

Wars between nations and civil wars are two of the main reasons why people become refugees. Civil wars are fought between people in the same country. Beginning in late 2013, a civil war in the African nation of South Sudan caused widespread destruction. By early 2014, the war had forced more than 200,000 people to flee their homes. While most of these refugees moved within South Sudan, many arrived in neighboring Uganda. The Ugandan government opened camps in which the refugees could live for a time.

Genocide is another reason why people become refugees. Genocide is the systematic murder of an entire **ethnic**, national, or religious group. One of the worst examples of genocide in recent history took place in 1994. During a period of about 100 days, between 500,000 and 800,000 people were killed in Rwanda, a country in Central Africa.

The genocide began after the assassination of Rwanda's president, Juvénal Habyarimana. He was a member of the Hutu ethnic group. Some Hutu blamed people who were Tutsi, another ethnic group, for the president's death. Hutu groups began killing large numbers of Tutsi. About 2 million people fled the conflict. About 80,000 people died in the refugee camps that were set up in neighboring countries. Many deaths resulted from unclean conditions in the overcrowded camps.

5 Internally Displaced Persons

Internally displaced persons, or IDPs, are people who have been forced to flee their homes but remain in their own country. They have not crossed an international border in search of safety. War is the main reason why a person becomes an IDP. Gunfire and bombs destroy homes and businesses. Warring groups may round up residents, even children, to fight as soldiers. People sometimes flee areas that their families have lived in for generations. In the South American country of Colombia, a civil war that began in the mid-1960s has created almost 5 million IDPs. Many have moved from the countryside to urban areas, where they live in poor housing and have trouble finding work.

In 2013, there were more than 28.8 million IDPs around the world. Almost one-fourth of them were in the Middle East country of Syria. They were forced from their homes by the civil war that began in 2011. Government troops fought against several groups trying to overthrow President Bashar al-Assad. By the end of 2013, there were 6.5 million IDPs in Syria, as well as 2.4 million refugees in other countries.

War is not the only reason why a person becomes an IDP. People are often displaced after a natural disaster. In 2011, for example, almost 15 million people were internally displaced because of several disasters, especially in Asia. These events included flooding in Thailand and a typhoon, or hurricane, in the Philippines. In addition, a powerful earthquake in Japan caused a tsunami, or wave of ocean water, that caused widespread flooding and damage.

Camps for displaced people in Syria often are crowded and can provide only small tents for shelter.

Should International Organizations and Wealthy Nations Help Care for Refugees?

Countries that receive refugees are known as host countries. Most of the refugees from Syria's civil war went to nearby host countries, such as Egypt, Lebanon, Jordan, Turkey, and Iraq. By early 2014, about 600,000 refugees had made their way to Jordan, accounting for 10 percent of that country's population. Providing food, shelter, and medical care to large numbers of refugees is very costly.

United Nations Officials

A major refugee crisis is a problem for the entire world. When so many people are displaced and suffering, it is right for international organizations to step in to help. These groups have experts who know how to deal with problems that occur in refugee camps.

Host Country Officials

We cannot afford to provide refugees with food, shelter, and medicine. The costs are too high. We also do not have the people to give the care that is needed. Wealthy nations and international organizations should step in to pay many of the costs.

Some National Leaders

We are sorry for the suffering of refugees in other parts of the world. However, we have our own problems at home that need to be taken care of and paid for. Providing aid to refugees elsewhere may mean that less money is available to solve problems in our own country.

Some Residents of Other Nations

With the help of international organizations, host countries should deal with their refugee problems. It should not be our responsibility to take in refugees. People from different cultures may not fit in well once they arrive in our country.

| For | Supportive | Undecided | Unsupportive | Against |

Global Immigration

KEY CONCEPTS

1 Immigration to North America

2 Immigration to Europe

3 Contributions of Immigrants

4 Problems Faced by Immigrants

5 Documented and
Undocumented Immigrants

Many cities in North America have neighborhoods called Chinatown, Little Italy, Germantown, or Little India. These are areas where many immigrants from certain countries chose to settle when they first arrived. The neighborhoods are examples of how diverse North America's population is as a result of immigration.

1 Immigration to North America

It is often said that the United States is a nation of immigrants. Even North America's original inhabitants came from somewhere else. Many scientists believe that, thousands of years ago, a land bridge connected northeastern Asia and northwestern North America. People from Asia walking across this land, which is now under water, may have been the first residents of North America. They could have been ancestors of the American Indians living throughout the continent when European settlers arrived.

Europeans began coming to North America in large numbers soon after the Italian explorer Christopher Columbus landed in the Bahamas in 1492. Immigrants from Spain and France arrived first. English and Dutch settlers followed. Some came to find a better life. Others came to freely practice their faith.

While most immigrants came willingly, others did not. From the 1600s to the 1800s, hundreds of thousands of Africans were brought to be slaves in North America. However, the largest North American migration was the Great Atlantic Migration that began in the 1800s.

During the 19th century, thousands of immigrants also came from China, Japan, and other countries in Asia. During the 1860s, Chinese workers played an important role in building the first transcontinental railroad, which connected the eastern United States with the West Coast. The Chinese immigrants often were paid less than other laborers and did some of the most dangerous work.

"Chinese workers helped build the first transcontinental railroad across America."

During the late 20th and early 21st centuries, the largest numbers of immigrants to the United States have come from Latin America and Asia. The greatest number of Latin American immigrants have arrived from Mexico. Many Asian immigrants are from the Philippines, India, Vietnam, and South Korea.

2 Immigration to Europe

In October 2013, nearly 400 African immigrants died when their ship went down off the Italian island of Lampedusa. Most were from Eritrea and Somalia. The disaster focused attention on immigrants coming to Europe.

Thousands of immigrants journey to Europe each year. Most settle in Germany, Great Britain, France, Spain, Italy, and the Netherlands. Some risk their lives.

Many of Europe's immigrants arrive from **developing countries**. Often, they are seeking opportunities to find work and earn more money. Some immigrants are escaping war or natural disasters. European countries tend to receive immigrants from nations they used to control. Many immigrants to France are from former French colonies in North and Central Africa. Geography is also a factor. Italy and Spain receive large numbers of immigrants because they are close to poor nations in Africa.

There is also a large amount of immigration within Europe itself. In recent years, many people have **emigrated** from Eastern Europe. In most cases, they are looking for higher-paying jobs in the wealthier countries of Western Europe.

Great Britain and Germany are two countries that have felt the impact of immigration the most. Germany has the strongest economy in Europe, so it attracts people from other continents and from Eastern Europe. In recent years, Germany has faced a shortage of workers in some professions, such as health care and engineering. It has been welcoming workers from Poland, the Czech Republic, Slovakia, and other Eastern European countries.

The number of European immigrants who came to Great Britain seeking work increased by 73 percent from 2011 to 2013. Wages are often higher in Great Britain than in other European countries. Many people arrived from Bulgaria and Romania, two of Europe's poorest nations.

Many of the boats carrying emigrants from Africa are small, severely overcrowded, and in poor condition.

Should Immigrant Children Be Taught in Their Native Language?

Often, immigrants move to countries where the language spoken is different from their native language. Immigrant children may enter school in their new country not knowing the language in which other children are being taught. People disagree about what is the best way to teach the new students to help them adapt most quickly to their new school and country.

Educational Researchers

Immigrant students should receive special lessons to learn the language of their new country. Until they learn it, however, they need to be taught certain subjects in their native language. These students will fall behind in such areas as math and science if they cannot receive instruction in a language they understand.

Some Local School Officials

Bilingual education is often the best solution for immigrant students. Receiving part of their instruction in the new language helps them learn that language faster. At the same time, receiving some instruction in their native language helps them better understand certain difficult subjects.

Some School Principals

We understand that it can be very hard for students to do well in school if they do not understand the language the teacher is using. However, some schools have immigrant students from many countries with different languages. We do not have teachers who know these languages or books written in them. We have to use only one language.

Some Politicians

Immigrant children need to learn the language of their new country as quickly as possible. If families have chosen to live in our country, then it is their responsibility to learn our language. That is the only way that they can become good citizens of the country where they now live.

| For | Supportive | Undecided | Unsupportive | Against |

3 Contributions of Immigrants

Immigrants make important contributions to their new countries. Many immigrants adapt, or adjust, quickly to the customs and way of life in the nation where they now live. At the same time, they keep some of the traditions of their native country. These traditions become part of their new country's culture. For example, in the United States, foods and ways of cooking that originated in other parts of the world are now popular with millions of Americans. People of all cultural backgrounds enjoy Mexican, Italian, Chinese, and many other types of restaurants.

Immigrants to the United States have contributed to science and the arts as well. Albert Einstein, one of the most important scientists of the 20th century, was an immigrant from Germany. Film director Ang Lee was born in Taiwan. He has won many awards for his movies, including the 2012 film *Life of Pi*. American architect I. M. Pei, who has designed well-known buildings in all parts of the world, is from China.

Immigrants also help a country's economy. In the United States, immigrants are more likely than native-born Americans to start a business. In fact, 18 percent of owners of small businesses are immigrants. People born in other countries have also helped develop some of the largest U.S. companies. The Kohl's department store chain started as a grocery store opened in Wisconsin by Polish immigrant Maxwell Kohl in the 1920s. Russian-born Sergey Brin was one of the founders of the technology company Google.

Immigrants may send some of their earnings to family members in their native countries. These payments, known as remittances, can be very helpful to family members living in poverty. They also add a great deal of money to the economies of developing nations. Remittances to people in developing countries totaled more than $400 billion in 2013.

The glass pyramid that is the main entrance to the Louvre Museum in Paris, France, was designed by I. M. Pei.

Immigrant children often attend special classes to learn their new country's language.

4 Problems Faced by Immigrants

Immigrants are not always welcomed in their new countries. Some people may dislike immigrants because they dress differently, speak other languages, or have different customs. These people may not want to see their own country's way of life changed by adding immigrant traditions. They may not want to hear different languages spoken in their communities.

Sometimes, people **stereotype** immigrant groups instead of seeing the newcomers as individuals. These stereotypes are often negative and not based on facts. For example, despite the labor of Chinese immigrants on the transcontinental railroad, some Americans in the 1800s believed that Chinese people would not work hard.

Immigrant children are often bullied in school because of their background. Children who have a hard time speaking the language of their new country often struggle to fit in. They may have trouble making friends.

Immigrants also may be victims of crimes motivated by stereotypes. This occurred after the September 11, 2001, terrorist attacks on the United States. The attackers were Arabs from the Middle East who were **Islamist extremists**. The terrorists flew planes into two skyscrapers in New York City and the military headquarters near Washington, D.C., called the Pentagon. Nearly 3,000 people died. Almost all Arabs and Muslims in the United States oppose terrorism, and many spoke out against the attacks. However, following September 11, 2001, crimes against Arab and Muslim immigrants in the United States increased.

5 Documented and Undocumented Immigrants

Most countries have immigration laws. These laws often set quotas, or limits, on the number of people who can immigrate to a country each year. There may be both a worldwide maximum and quotas for individual nations.

Countries usually require immigrants, before they enter, to obtain **visas** that allow them to live in their new nation permanently. Immigration laws often describe the process for obtaining such documents. These laws also usually set the rules for how immigrants can, after a period of time, become citizens of their new countries.

Immigrants who enter a country without obtaining the proper type of visa are known as undocumented or illegal immigrants. Sometimes, undocumented immigrants have no papers at all. They simply try to cross a nation's border without getting caught. It is estimated that, in the 1990s and early 2000s, millions of Mexican and Central American undocumented immigrants entered the United States from Mexico. They often made a difficult journey across remote deserts, and thousands of people may have died. In many cases, the immigrants were seeking opportunities to work and earn more money than they could in their home countries.

Some illegal immigrants obtain a type of visa that allows them to enter a country for a limited period of time. These kinds of visas may be given to tourists, people who travel abroad for business, or students coming to a country to attend college. However, some people simply stay past the date by which they are required to leave. This type of illegal immigration to the United States has also been common in recent years. Overall, an estimated 11.7 undocumented immigrants were living in the United States in 2012.

Number of Undocumented Immigrants in the United States, 1990–2012

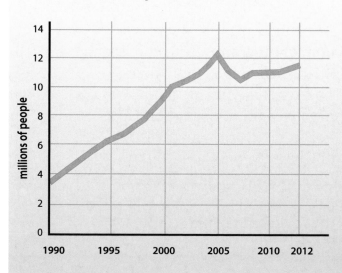

Should the United States Allow Undocumented Immigrants to Stay in the Country Legally?

Amnesty is a decision by a government not to punish people for breaking the law. There has been a great deal of debate in the United States in recent years about whether there should be some type of amnesty program for illegal immigrants. Bills to provide a "path to citizenship" have been introduced in Congress. However, there is also strong opposition.

Immigration Reform Advocates

Undocumented immigrants are living, working, and going to school all over the United States. They help their communities and have made new lives for themselves. We have to find a way for them to remain in the country legally.

Law Enforcement Officials

It is impossible to find and arrest all the millions of illegal immigrants to send them back to their native countries. Most of these people have not committed any crimes after entering the United States. We should use our efforts to catch the few who break the law while living here.

Some Citizens

Granting amnesty will make the U.S. immigration problem worse. It will encourage even more people to enter the country illegally. These immigrants will compete with citizens for jobs.

Some Politicians

We are a nation of laws. Undocumented immigrants have broken the law and should not receive amnesty. There should be greater efforts to arrest people in the country illegally and to guard the nation's borders to keep out new immigrants.

For   Supportive   Undecided   Unsupportive   Against

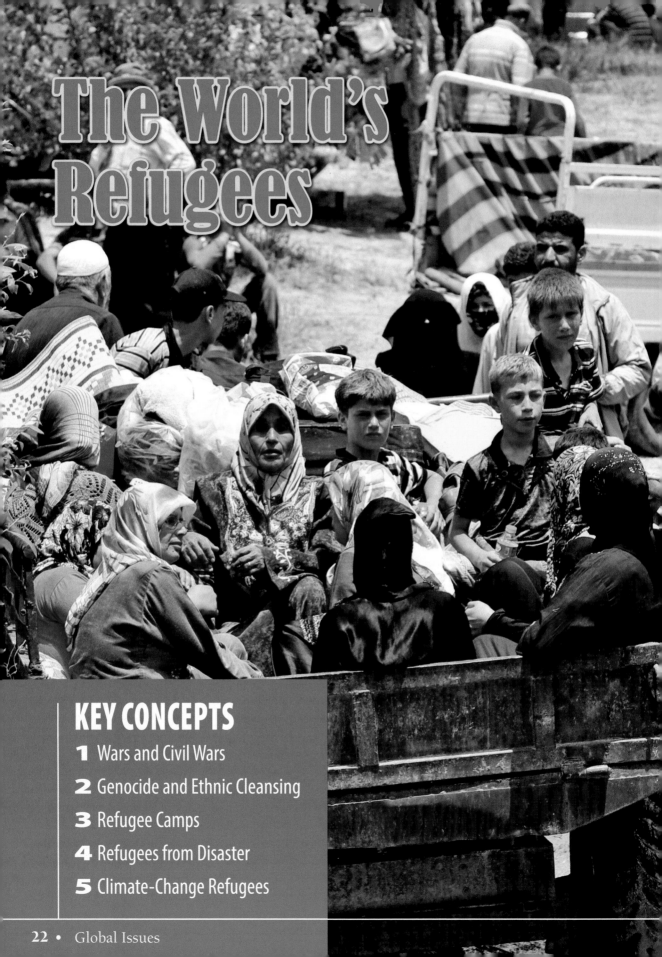

The World's Refugees

KEY CONCEPTS

Pictures of people displaced by war or a natural disaster are often shown by the news media. People move slowly along crowded roads, carrying the few possessions they could take with them. Some people ride packed into cars or trucks. Others walk. All are seeking shelter, safety, and food.

1 Wars and Civil Wars

In the 20th century, combat airplanes, missiles, and more powerful weapons of many kinds were developed. As a result, civilians became victims of war in larger numbers than ever before. During World War II (1939–1945), more than 10 million people were displaced. Bombing heavily damaged large parts of many European cities, destroying millions of homes. Recovery from the conflict took time. Six years after the war ended, the United Nations estimated that 1 million people still waited to return home.

Since 1945, no war has been as widespread or deadly as World War II. However, many other conflicts have created millions of new refugees. For example, fighting in Afghanistan began in 2001, when the United States sent troops to the country to help remove a government that supported Islamist terrorists. In 2013, there were 2.6 million refugees of the Afghanistan war. Most were in Pakistan and Iran. Another

"Since 1945, many conflicts have created millions of war refugees."

574,000 people were IDPs inside Afghanistan. Worldwide, the number of war refugees and IDPs was about 45 million.

The United Nations was established in 1945 to help promote peace and cooperation among nations. Since that time, the UN has played a leading role in providing housing, medical care, and food to refugees around the world. Many nongovernmental organizations, or NGOs, also assist war refugees. These groups include the International Committee of the Red Cross and Médecins Sans Frontières, or Doctors Without Borders.

Children are often the victims of war. The United Nations Children's Fund, or UNICEF, reported that about 2 million children were killed in wars fought during the 1990s. Another 6 million were seriously injured or disabled. An additional 12 million children became homeless.

2 Genocide and Ethnic Cleansing

The Holocaust during World War II is one of the deadliest instances of genocide in world history. As soon as Adolf Hitler's Nazi party came to power in Germany in 1933, the government began to persecute Jews. Their property was taken, and their rights were limited. As the 1930s went on, a growing number of Jews were arrested and held in camps known as concentration camps. Members of other cultural groups were also held in the camps. People thought to be opponents of the government were imprisoned as well. However, the largest numbers of inmates were Jews.

In the early years of World War II, Germany conquered other countries in Europe. Jews in those countries were sent to concentration camps as well, and arrests of Jews in Germany increased. In some camps, inmates were forced to work until they died from the harsh conditions.

By 1942, Germany was using a number of camps for the large-scale killing of Jews and other inmates. In these so-called death camps, thousands of people were often killed in one day. By the time Germany was defeated in 1945, as many as 6 million Jews had lost their lives.

Genocide, also known as ethnic cleansing, occurred again in Europe nearly half a century after World War II. The country of Yugoslavia was made up of six regions. The Serbian ethnic group was the largest in the country. However, there were large non-Serbian populations in some areas, including Croatia and Bosnia-Herzegovina. In the early 1990s, these areas declared their independence. Serbian army units and other Serbian groups launched attacks against non-Serbians, especially Bosnian Muslims. By the time the fighting ended in 1995, this ethnic cleansing had resulted in the death of about 100,000 people.

Yugoslavia's former president Slobodan Milosevic was put on trial by an international court for his government's ethnic cleansing policies.

Do Countries Have a Responsibility to Use Their Armed Forces to Prevent Genocide?

In 1948, the UN General Assembly approved the Convention for the Prevention and Punishment of the Crimes of Genocide. This document called on all nations to prevent and punish acts of genocide in war and peacetime. Since then, genocide has taken place in several areas around the world, including Bosnia-Herzegovina and Rwanda. Often, other countries have not taken strong action to stop the killing.

Human Rights Activists

The world's nations have a moral obligation to act when large numbers of people are being killed because of their cultural group. Countries with strong military forces should use them to save lives. Events such as the ethnic cleansing in Bosnia-Herzegovina cannot be allowed to happen again.

UN Officials

Members of the United Nations should follow the organization's policies, including taking action to stop genocide. This is required by international law. The UN can help countries to act together to prevent this type of killing.

Some Concerned Parents

We agree that genocide is a terrible tragedy. However, we do not support sending our troops to a foreign country. These soldiers are our children. They may be killed or injured in a war that is none of our concern.

Some Political Leaders

The purpose of the armed forces is to protect our country. Genocide in a foreign nation that has not threatened our country is not our business. We should not spend money or commit troops to interfere in the internal problems of other nations.

For	Supportive	Undecided	Unsupportive	Against

Mapping the World's Refugees

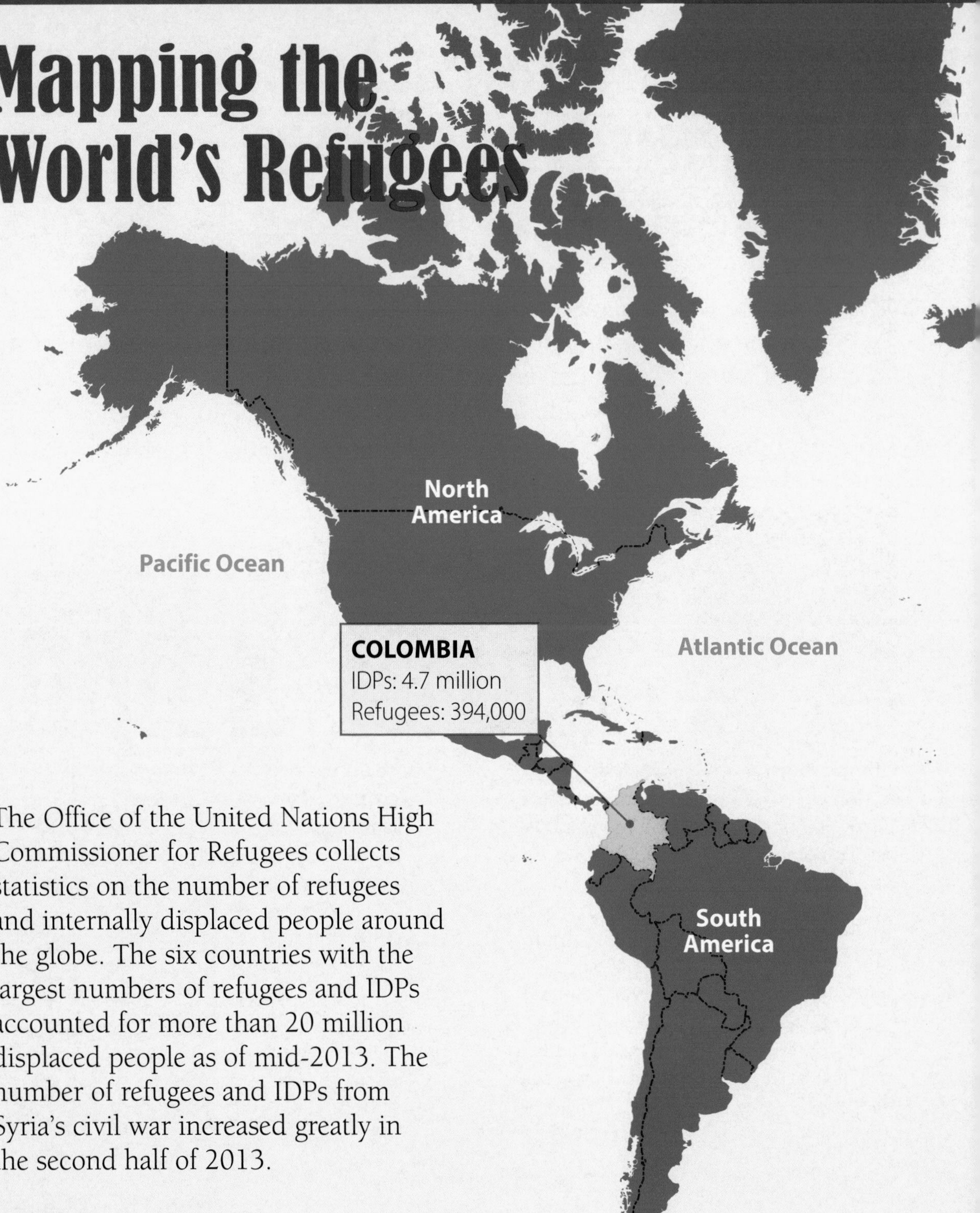

North America

Pacific Ocean

Atlantic Ocean

COLOMBIA
IDPs: 4.7 million
Refugees: 394,000

South America

The Office of the United Nations High Commissioner for Refugees collects statistics on the number of refugees and internally displaced people around the globe. The six countries with the largest numbers of refugees and IDPs accounted for more than 20 million displaced people as of mid-2013. The number of refugees and IDPs from Syria's civil war increased greatly in the second half of 2013.

Legend

☐ Countries with the largest numbers of displaced people

SYRIA
IDPs: 4.3 million
Refugees: 1.9 million

IRAQ
IDPs: 993,000
Refugees: 409,000

AFGHANISTAN
IDPs: 574,000
Refugees: 2.6 million

SUDAN
IDPs: 1.9 million
Refugees: 632,000

SOMALIA
IDPs: 1.1 million
Refugees: 1.1 million

Arctic Ocean

Europe

Asia

Africa

Pacific Ocean

Indian Ocean

Australia

Southern Ocean

N
W E
S

SCALE
1,200 Miles
1,200 Kilometers

3 Refugee Camps

The camps set up to receive and care for refugees fleeing war or other disasters can be difficult places to live. Often, a country near the nation in crisis will build camps, as thousands of refugees start crossing its border. The United Nations and NGOs also establish refugee camps and help care for the people in them. These people often live in overcrowded conditions.

If a war continues for some time, camps may receive far more refugees than they were meant to hold. The camps try to provide food, safe drinking water, tents, bedding, and medical care. Often they cannot supply enough. Most camps are intended to be short-term places to stay until refugees can return home. However, some camps remain open for many years. Long-term camps create a need for schools, sturdier housing, and other types of services that can be costly and difficult to provide.

More than 20 years ago, the United Nations High Commissioner for Refugees opened a refugee camp in the small town of Dadaab, Kenya. It was supposed to house 90,000 people fleeing from civil war in Somalia. Today, more than 332,000 people call the camp home. It is the largest refugee camp in the world.

In the early months of 2013, about 10,000 refugees from the Central African Republic (CAR) and 30,000 from West Darfur, an area in Sudan, fled into Chad. Both groups were escaping from civil war in their home countries. Chad has a policy of accepting and aiding refugees. A total of 12 camps were set up there for Sudanese and 5 camps for people from the CAR. By the end of 2013, these camps were home to nearly 350,000 Sudanese and more than 74,000 CAR refugees.

Chad has received refugees from conflict in Sudan for a number of years.

4 Refugees from Disaster

Floods, fires, volcanic eruptions, earthquakes, avalanches, mudslides, and storms occur all the time. When natural disasters such as these cause heavy damage in a region, large numbers of people can be left homeless. The number of refugees created by natural disasters is small when compared to the number resulting from war and other causes. However, in 2012, more than 32 million people fled their homes because of weather-related and other natural disasters.

One of the worst North American disasters in recent years occurred when Hurricane Sandy struck the East Coast 2012. The storm caused at least $50 billion in damage in the United States. Hundreds of thousands of homes were destroyed or seriously damaged, forcing many people to find shelter elsewhere.

Wealthier countries are somewhat better able to cope with the costs of such a crisis. Poor countries are not able to bear these costs. In 2010, a massive earthquake struck Haiti, the poorest country in the Western Hemisphere. Three years after the disaster, hundreds of thousands of displaced people still lived in tents.

Low-lying areas close to seacoasts or large rivers may be at high risk for floods when a storm strikes. These disasters can leave many thousands of people homeless within a single day. In November 2013, one of the strongest storms ever recorded, Typhoon Haiyan, slammed into the Philippines. The storm killed more than 4,000 Filipinos and displaced about 4.4 million people.

When Typhoon Ketsana struck the Philippines in 2009, there was widespread flooding and thousands of homes were destroyed.

5 Climate-Change Refugees

Many scientists believe that powerful storms and other natural disasters may become more common as a result of climate change. These scientists see evidence that Earth is going through a period of **global warming**. As the world's population grows, the number of people living in areas at high risk for flood or storm damage also increases. Some experts believe that future disasters could cause hundreds of millions of people to leave their homes.

Climate-change refugees affect not only their home countries but neighboring areas as well. As large-scale migrations takes place, food and water shortages may occur. Disease can spread quickly as areas the refugees move to become more crowded. The costs of caring for the refugees can be huge.

Scientists point out that global warming is causing ice to melt in regions near the North and South Poles. The melting ice is raising sea levels around the world. If this trend continues, some low-lying coastal areas may be covered by ocean water in the future. The people living in such areas will have to move. In Bangladesh, much of the land is less than 33 feet (10 meters) above sea level. The country has more than 160 million people. Some experts believe that, in a few decades, large areas of the country may be under water. Tens of millions of people may become refugees.

Weather changes produced by global warming also include reduced rainfall in some areas. Climate change may create long-lasting droughts. Droughts can destroy crops and reduce drinking water supplies. In the future, widespread food and water shortages in some regions, including parts of Africa, may create millions of new refugees.

Droughts in Somalia have already caused many people seeking food and water to become refugees.

Should Countries Do More to Prevent Global Warming?

In the opinion of many scientists, human activity is a main cause of global warming. Gases such as carbon dioxide in Earth's atmosphere trap some of the Sun's heat reaching the planet. Carbon dioxide is naturally present in the atmosphere. However, when people burn **fossil fuels**, such as coal, gasoline, and other products made from oil, carbon dioxide is produced. As a result, the amount of this gas in the atmosphere is increasing. Some people disagree with the view that carbon dioxide **emissions** are important in producing climate change.

Climate Scientists
The scientific evidence is clear that people's use of fossil fuels is changing Earth's climate. If we do not find ways to reduce carbon dioxide emissions, many millions of people will not be able to remain in their homelands. It is a responsibility of citizens all over the world to avoid such a disaster.

Some Government Officials
To reduce the use of fossil fuels, other forms of energy must take their place. These include solar, wind, and water power. Government programs are providing aid to develop these energy sources. However, there is a limit to the amount of money governments can spend.

Skeptical Citizens
We need our cars to get to work and drive our children to school. Changing the way we heat our house can cost thousands of dollars. Before people make major changes in their way of life, the evidence that humans are causing global warming must be stronger. Perhaps it is a natural change.

Factory Owners
If the government forces businesses to stop or greatly reduce their use of fossil fuels, companies such as mine will have to close. Jobs will be lost. We cannot afford to hurt our economy today because of what might happen to the climate at some time in the future.

For   Supportive   Undecided   Unsupportive   Against

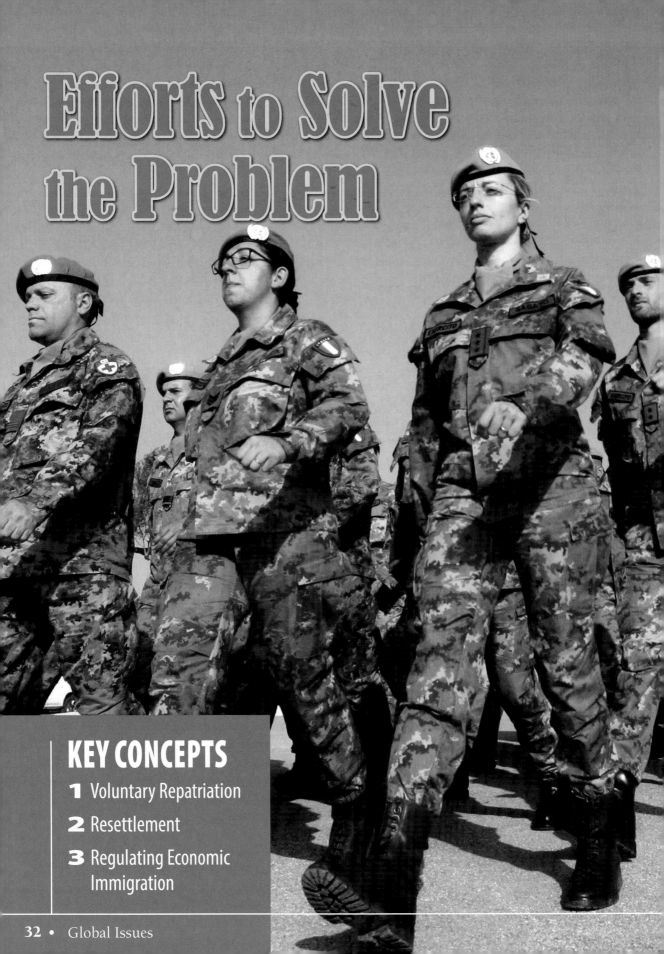

Efforts to Solve the Problem

KEY CONCEPTS

1 Voluntary Repatriation

2 Resettlement

3 Regulating Economic Immigration

inding solutions to problems caused by migration can be difficult. Many refugees may wish to return to their homelands, but this may not be possible. For some refugees, it may be necessary to help them find new homes in other areas.

1 Voluntary Repatriation

The Universal Declaration of Human Rights was agreed to in 1948 by the members of the United Nations. Article 13 of the document states, "Everyone has the right to leave any country, including his own, and to return to his country." Voluntary repatriation is the process by which a displaced person returns to his or her region of origin. Before war refugees can repatriate, however, the situation inside their homeland must be safe.

In some nations, such as Sudan, civil wars or other violence continue for years. The UN often works to settle disputes. It may help the warring parties negotiate a settlement. UN peacekeeping troops may be sent into a country to keep opposing forces separated and help make sure civilians are safe.

If a government is engaged in ethnic cleansing, the UN may organize actions by its members against that government. These actions may include stopping trade or other dealings with the government engaged in violence. Sometimes, these efforts are successful. In other cases, they are not.

2 Resettlement

Sometimes, refugees cannot return home. That means they have to start their lives over again in another country. From 1975 to 2013, the United States admitted more than 3 million refugees.

Almost half of the refugees came from Southeast Asia. In the 1960s and 1970s, the United States fought in the Vietnam War. After U.S. troops left, the forces that had opposed the United States won the war. Many people in Vietnam, Cambodia, and Laos who had sided with the United States now felt unsafe.

UN Peacekeeping Missions

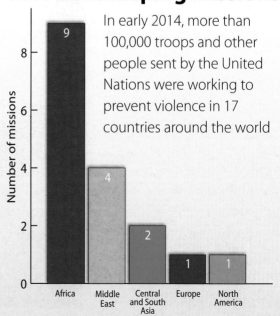

In early 2014, more than 100,000 troops and other people sent by the United Nations were working to prevent violence in 17 countries around the world

3 Regulating Economic Immigration

When people feel that there is little chance of improving their lives in their own country, they may seek a better life somewhere else. Whenever poorer countries are located near a wealthier one, people from the poorer nations tend to emigrate looking for jobs. This has been the case for many undocumented immigrants coming from Mexico and Central America to the United States.

Some Americans believe that undocumented workers harm the U.S. economy. These workers may be willing to accept very low wages. As a result, they help companies keep wages low for all of their workers. Some research has found that undocumented workers in the United States lowered the wages of citizens who did not have a high-school diploma. Other research has concluded, however, that in states with many immigrants, undocumented workers did not compete with skilled workers who were citizens.

In recent years, the United States has taken a number of steps to reduce illegal immigration. The U.S. government has built hundreds of miles (kilometers) of fencing along the border with Mexico to keep immigrants from crossing. It has also sharply increased the number of law enforcement officers patrolling the border to catch immigrants.

The United States has also signed trade agreements with Mexico and the countries of Central America. These agreements make it easier for U.S. companies to sell goods in Mexico and Central America. They also help companies in those countries to sell their goods in the United States. Some people who favor such trade agreements believe they will increase job opportunities in Mexico and Central America. As a result, fewer workers may feel a need to leave their home countries to find jobs.

A steel fence 18 feet (5.5 meters) high separates Nogales, Mexico, from the U.S. state of Arizona.

Do Governments Have a Right to Refuse Entry to Economic Immigrants?

Many nations, including the United States and European countries, have laws that regulate immigration. People who favor such laws believe countries must be able to control who enters in order to protect their economies and citizens. Other people favor greater freedom of movement for job seekers.

Anti-immigration Activists
There are a limited number of jobs in the country. There are unemployed citizens looking for work. It is the duty of the government to control the migration of people from other countries who will compete for jobs.

Government Immigration Officials
The government has a right to control its borders. This is a matter of safety as well as economics. Immigration laws require people who want to enter the country to provide information about their backgrounds. People who are criminals or may be a threat to the country can be kept out.

Human Rights Advocates
People facing extreme poverty in their homelands may need help just as much as people in a country at war. It is understandable for citizens not to want greater competition for jobs. However, wealthier countries have a duty to provide opportunities for people who are poor and suffering.

Immigration Activists
Immigrants seeking jobs can be a great help to a country. They are willing to work hard. They bring their talents and skills with them. Some of these people may make important contributions to their new country. They should be welcomed.

For   Supportive   Undecided   Unsupportive   Against

Migrants and Refugees through History

People have moved from one place to another for centuries. The reasons are as varied as the people themselves. Today, humans are still on the move, whether by choice or because they are forced. Whatever their reason, migrants are searching for a better life.

About 8,000 BC

According to many scientists, the first people to live in North America migrate from Asia over a land bridge connecting the two continents at that time. Their **descendants** spread out to populate the entire region.

1619 AD

The first African slaves arrive in the present-day United States. Over the next 200 years, hundreds of thousands of African slaves will be shipped to the area.

1717–1775

More than 250,000 Irish and Scottish people emigrate to America, many of them to escape **famine**.

1845–1850

1845–1850

The Great Potato Famine, when crops rot in the fields, sends hundreds of thousands of Irish immigrants to live in the United States.

1914–1918

Millions of people are displaced in Eastern Europe by World War I.

1939–1945

More than 10 million people are displaced by World War II.

1950–1993

About 3 million ethnic Germans immigrate to Germany, most of them from Poland, Russia, and other nearby countries.

1956

During Algeria's war for independence from France, tens of thousands of people flee to Tunisia and Morocco.

1956

1960s

Many nations in Central and Southern Africa gain their independence from Great Britain, France, and other European countries. The changes in government lead to widespread movement of people throughout the region.

1977

Warfare begins in northeastern Africa, and as many as 3 million Somalis and Ethiopians are displaced. A year later, the UNHCR begins an assistance program for Ethiopian refugees in neighboring countries.

1984

Famine in Ethiopia kills hundreds of thousands of people. Many more flee to Sudan, Somalia, and Djibouti.

1989

A political settlement ends South Africa's occupation of Namibia, and 45,000 Namibians return home. Civil war starts in Liberia, The conflict uproots 700,000 people.

1992

A peace agreement ends a long civil war in the African nation of Mozambique. About 1.7 million refugees return home in one of the most successful repatriation programs since the end of World War II.

1997

Violence increases in Sierra Leone's civil war. More than 400,000 people flee the African nation as rebels battle government forces. The UN helps end the fighting in the early 2000s.

2003–2011

Years of warfare following the U.S.-led invasion of Iraq result in more than 2 million Iraqi refugees leaving the country.

2011

Syria's civil war begins. By the end of 2013, almost 9 million Syrians are IDPs or refugees in other countries, including Jordan, Lebanon, and Turkey.

2013

Worldwide, an estimated 45 million people are refugees or IDPs.

2011

Working on Migrant and Refugee Issues

AID WORKER

Duties Distribute aid to people who are victims of war or natural disasters

Education College-level education is not necessary, but having practical skills and being in good physical condition are helpful

Interest Wanting to help people in need, travel

Aid workers often must do their jobs in dangerous areas, where fighting is taking place. Some workers help people in refugee camps. Others work within communities. Their work may involve distributing food, providing first aid, helping to put up housing, and giving school lessons to children. Aid workers need to quickly assess emergencies and decide what is needed most. Often, they are employed by international organizations or government agencies.

ENGLISH AS A SECOND LANGUAGE TEACHER

Duties Teach English to adults or children whose main language is not English

Education A bachelor's or master's degree

Interest Helping students succeed in work, school, and the community

English as a second language, or ESL, teachers in the United States work in a variety of settings to help immigrants or refugees from other areas learn English. Some teachers work with adults and others with children. Teachers may be employed by public schools, colleges, language schools for adults, or companies with many non-English-speaking workers. Some teachers are self-employed and give lessons to individual students. ESL teachers use a range of books and electronic materials to teach English.

SOCIAL WORKER

Duties Provide support to individuals who survived difficult experiences or are adjusting to a new way of life

Education A bachelor's or master's degree

Interest Helping people deal with problems

Social workers may work in a wide range of settings to help immigrants or refugees who are resettling in a new country. Government agencies and private organizations working with immigrants and refugees may employ social workers. Some social workers focus on providing assistance with practical aspects of life, such as adjusting to a new community or a new school. Others may assist people in dealing with emotional problems they may have as a result of events they lived through or the stress of making a new life in a different country.

IMMIGRATION OFFICIAL

Duties To carry out and enforce immigration laws

Education A high school or college degree

Interest Ensuring that laws are obeyed and people are treated fairly

Immigration officials are government employees who carry out a nation's immigration laws and make sure these laws are enforced fairly. Some people are involved in guarding borders. Others check documents of people entering the country. Some jobs include researching and analyzing immigration applications. Officials often also interview migrants and refugees to make sure they are telling the truth about their lives and countries of origin. Some officials have the power to grant or deny applications. At times, immigration officials work with other government agencies.

Key Migrant and Refugee Organizations

UNHCR

Goal Lead and coordinate international action to protect refugees and solve their problems

Reach Global

Facts Has a staff of nearly 8,000 people in more than 125 countries

The Office of the United Nations High Commissioner for Refugees (UNHCR) is the main refugee agency of the United Nations. It was established in 1950 by the UN General Assembly to help people displaced by World War II. It has helped victims of many conflicts since then. The UNHCR protects million of people who have become homeless. It provides food, clean water, health care, education, and other services to refugees. It also studies how much money and aid are needed to deal with a refugee crisis, and it urges governments and others to make donations.

AMNESTY INTERNATIONAL

Goal To end human rights abuses

Reach Global

Facts 3 million supporters in 150 countries

Amnesty International is an independent organization without connections to any government. It holds no political or religious beliefs. The organization was formed in 1961. It is funded by donations from its members and other individuals. The group works to protect basic human rights for people in countries all over the world. These rights include freedom from punishment for one's beliefs or for being a member of any cultural group. Amnesty International works to support and gain the release of people unfairly arrested by governments. It opposes cruel treatment of people in prison.

NNIRR

Goal Protect the right of all immigrants in the United States regardless of whether they are documented or not

Reach United States

Facts Helped start an international organization to protect migrants' rights

The National Network for Immigrant and Refugee Rights (NNIRR) works to ensure fair treatment for immigrants in the United States. Established in 1986, the organization opposes any violation of people's right if they are arrested under U.S. immigration laws. It advocates for allowing undocumented immigrants to remain in the United States.

ICRC

Goal Provide assistance to lessen human suffering, protect people's lives and health, and help people who are victims of conflict or a natural disaster

Reach Global

Facts Largest **humanitarian** organization in the world

The International Committee of the Red Cross (ICRC) was created in 1863 to provide assistance to the victims of war. Today, its mission is varied. The ICRC visits people who have been imprisoned during war. The agency tries to make sure that these prisoners are not treated cruelly. The ICRC also helps families displaced by war, including by helping them find work. The agency distributes food and household items, and it provides health care for those in need.

Research a Migration Issue

The Issue

Many people have different opinions about immigration issues. For example, people disagree about whether undocumented immigrants should be given amnesty. They hold different views about whether citizens of a country should have to compete with immigrants for jobs. Before discussing or debating such topics, it is important to hear all points of view. Discussing issues will make sure that the actions taken are beneficial for all involved.

Get the Facts

Choose an issue (Political, Cultural, Economic, or Ecological) from this book. Then, pick one of the four points of view presented in the issue spectrum. Using this book and researching in the library or the Internet, find out more about the group you chose. What is important to the group? Why is it backing or opposing a particular policy? What claims or facts can it use to support its point of view? Be sure to write clear and concise supporting arguments for your group. Focus on its point of view. Will this group be affected in a positive or negative way by changes in the policy?

Use the Concept Web

A concept web is a useful research tool. Read the information and review the structure in the concept web on the next page. Use the relationships between concepts to help you understand your group's point of view.

Organize Your Research

Sort your information into organized points. Make sure your research answers clearly what impact the issue will have on your chosen group, how that impact will affect it, and why the group has chosen its specific point of view.

MIGRATION CONCEPT WEB

Use this concept web to understand the network of factors relating to migrant and refugee issues.

- Many come from developing countries
- Can return home
- Seek job opportunities and a better life for their families

- Have not obtained government permission to enter their new country
- Violate immigration laws
- May live and work in their new country for years
- Seek amnesty to stay in their new country

- Displaced by storms, floods, earthquakes, or other such events
- Many millions of people live in high-risk areas
- Number of victims may increase as a result of global warming

Economic Migrants

Undocumented Immigrants

Victims of Natural Disasters

MIGRANTS AND REFUGEES

Victims of Persecution

Victims of War

Forced Migrants

- May immigrate to practice their religion freely
- May wish to avoid harsh treatment based on race or cultural group

- Lose their homes during armed conflicts
- Find shelter in refugee camps in other countries
- May be internally displaced persons in their home country
- Warfare may go on for many years

- Has occurred many times in world history
- African slaves brought to North America
- American Indians sent to reservations
- European Jews sent to concentration camps

Test Your Knowledge

Answer each of the questions below to test your knowledge of migrants and refugees.

1 What is the name for the migration of millions of Europeans to North America in the 1800s and early 1900s?

2 What is the term for people forced to flee their homes because of wars or natural disasters?

3 In what year did the first African slaves arrive in the present-day United States?

4 What is the term for the killing of an entire ethnic, national, or religious group?

5 What was the killing of European Jews by Nazi Germany called?

6 About how many undocumented immigrants are living in the United States?

7 What word describes the decision by a government not to punish people for breaking the law?

8 Which country's civil war had displaced almost 9 million people by the end of 2013?

9 From what region did many people resettle in the United States beginning in 1975?

10 What term describes the process by which refugees return to their place of origin?

ANSWERS 1. The Great Atlantic Migration **2.** Refugees **3.** 1619 **4.** Genocide **5.** The Holocaust **6.** 11.7 million **7.** Amnesty **8.** Syria **9.** Southeast Asia **10.** Voluntary repatriation

1

2

5

7

8

Key Words

asylum: protection from danger given by a government to someone who has fled from another country

bilingual: using two languages

descendants: people related to a group that lived in an earlier time

developed countries: countries that have strong economies and advanced industries

developing countries: countries with low average income that until recently had little manufacturing and technology

emigrated: left one's native country to go elsewhere to live and work

emissions: gases or other substances released into the air

ethnic: relating to groups sharing cultural traits

famine: a severe shortage of food

fossil fuels: substances used to provide energy that are formed underground from plant or animal remains

globalization: being connected worldwide or, at least, over a large area of the world

global warming: an increase in average temperatures worldwide and related changes in weather conditions over a long period of time

Holocaust: the killing of millions of Jewish people and others by Germany's Nazi government during World War II

humanitarian: showing concern for the welfare of others

intolerance: unwillingness to accept people who hold different beliefs and views

Islamist extremists: religious terrorists who follow a code of conduct based on a literal reading of the Koran, Islam's holy book

persecution: being treated unfairly or cruelly, often because of one's race, religion, or cultural group

reservations: land set aside for special reasons, especially in North America for the use of American Indians

rural: relating to areas located outside cities and their suburbs

stereotype: to have a fixed idea that all people from a particular group are the same

visas: official papers that allow people to enter or travel through a specific country or region

Index

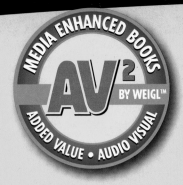

Log on to www.av2books.com

AV² by Weigl brings you media enhanced books that support active learning. Go to www.av2books.com, and enter the special code found on page 2 of this book. You will gain access to enriched and enhanced content that supplements and complements this book. Content includes video, audio, weblinks, quizzes, a slide show, and activities.

AV² Online Navigation

Audio
Listen to sections of the book read aloud.

Book Pages
AV² pages directly correspond to pages in the book.

Video
Watch informative video clips.

Key Words
Study vocabulary, and complete a matching word activity.

Embedded Weblinks
Gain additional information for research.

Quizzes
Test your knowledge.

Slide Show
View images and captions, and prepare a presentation.

Try This!
Complete activities and hands-on experiments.

AV² was built to bridge the gap between print and digital. We encourage you to tell us what you like and what you want to see in the future.

Sign up to be an AV² Ambassador at www.av2books.com/ambassador.

Due to the dynamic nature of the Internet, some of the URLs and activities provided as part of AV² by Weigl may have changed or ceased to exist. AV² by Weigl accepts no responsibility for any such changes. All media enhanced books are regularly monitored to update addresses and sites in a timely manner. Contact AV² by Weigl at 1-866-649-3445 or av2books@weigl.com with any questions, comments, or feedback.